CW00816111

MEMORIES OF LEISURE TIME FROM THE 1950s & 1960s

For Christine and Margaret,
who still enjoy a girls day out

Published in 2019 by
Pictures to Share Community Interest Company,
a UK based social enterprise that publishes
illustrated books for older people.

www.picturestoshare.co.uk

ISBN 978-0-9934049-5-5

Front Cover:
Family Time, May 1958: Joan Evans watches television with her husband and four children at their new home in the new town of Harlow, Essex. Photo by Frank Martin / BIPs / Getty Images.

Front endpaper:
Mother and two daughters sitting by fountain at holiday camp in Wales. Credit: Simon Kirwan / Getty

Rear endpaper:
West Ham Match, Young West Ham supporters at a match in the East End of London, 1960s.
Photo by Steve Lewis / Getty Images.

Title page:
Two men playing chess game, Contributor: ClassicStock / Alamy Stock Photo.

MEMORIES OF LEISURE TIME FROM THE 1950s & 1960s

Edited by Michelle Forster

Piggy Back Race

In the 1950s and early 1960s the holiday camp industry thrived. There were over 200 holiday camps in the UK.

Many working adults only got two weeks paid holiday a year. They often had to take their holiday at a time determined by their employer. Most factories had a closedown period in August and this would be the only time families could go on holiday.

A couple enjoying a piggy back race at a Butlin's holiday camp, 1953.
Photo by Bert Hardy / Picture Post / Getty Images.

For every great man doing a great job, there's a great woman telling him how to do it!

Leslie Deakins with his wife Norah working in the garden of their home, 1966.

Contributor: Trinity Mirror / Mirrorpix / Alamy Stock Photo.

Stamp collecting and football cards was a very popular hobby in the 1950s.

The hobby of collecting includes seeking, locating, acquiring, organising, cataloging, displaying, storing, and maintaining items that are of interest to an individual collector.

Stamp Collecting 1960s. Contributor: Chronicle / Alamy Stock Photo

Cigarette Cards; "Hints on Association Football" John Player and Sons, 1934. Contributor: PjrStudio / Alamy Stock Photo.

Singalong

Pubs in the UK could only open for 8 hours per day and only 5 hours on Sundays. The majority of pubs had pianos where regular customers would play and singalongs were a regular occurrence, with everyone joining in.

A group of people enjoy a sing-along at a pub in Birmingham, January 1961.
Photo by Bert Hardy Advertising Archive / Getty Images.

The popularity of music in the 1950s and 1960s ensured that the record player was just as popular as the radio.

They were always referred to as **"record players"**; to use the old-fashioned term **"gramophone"** in the late 50s and 60s marked you out as a member of the square, older generation.

Two teenage girls in curlers dreamily listening to 45 RPM records on a vintage record player at home in the 1950s. Contributor: Mira / Alamy Stock Photo.

Collection of 1960's 7" vinyl singles. Contributor: Marc Tielemans / Alamy Stock Photo.

Westinghouse
WESTINGHOUSE
M-G-M

British families enjoyed days out at the seaside on the beach, whatever the weather. You would find families sheltering behind windbreaks, in their Sunday best.

The adults would relax in deckchairs and the children would play ball, build sandcastles, go rock pooling and paddle in the sea. Some families rented beach huts by the day or week; these were great places to shelter from the rain and for changing into their swimming costumes.

The Lemm family of Castleford, Yorkshire, sitting behind their windbreaker on Blackpool Beach, 6th August 1961.
B/W photo / Blackpool, Lancashire, UK / © Mirrorpix / Bridgeman Images.

England's 1966 World Cup triumph is Britain's most watched TV broadcast.

More than 32.3 million saw the 4-2 extra-time win over West Germany at Wembley - even though only 15 million homes had a TV set.

England captain Bobby Moore 'chaired' by his team with the Jules Rimet Cup... after receiving it from the Queen after England won the Cup final 4 goals to 2, against West Germany. Credit: Bettmann / Contributor / Getty.

In the 1950s and 1960s it cost
2 shillings to go to the cinema.
This around £2.50 in today's money.

The National Anthem was played
at the end of the film. Some people
would stand or sing along as it was
played to show their patriotism.
Others would grab their coats and
make a mad dash for the door as the
film credits came up so as not to
endure the song.

THE GOOD, THE BAD AND THE UGLY Poster for 1966 PEA film with
Clint Eastwood. Contributor: Pictorial Press Ltd / Alamy Stock Photo.

A poster for Cecil B. DeMille's 1956 drama 'The Ten Commandments' starring
Charlton Heston and Yul Brynner. Photo by Movie Poster Image Art/Getty Images.

The Good, The Bad, and The Ugly was one of the most popular films of the 1960s.

The Ten Commandments was one of the most popular films of the 1950s.

Clothes were often homemade in the 1950s and 1960s, either sewn or knitted. Knitted items when outgrown were re-cycled by being unravelled and re-knitted into something else.

When collars on shirts became frayed, they were unpicked, turned inside out and sewed back on. All buttons and zips from old clothes were saved for the button box. Socks and stockings were darned.

Mother teaching daughter how to sew using a sewing machine, 1960.
Contributor: ClassicStock / Alamy Stock Photo.

SINGER

This is a party of workers from a factory in Leicester going to London for a day trip. It was common for employers to put on trips for their workers.

Passengers on a bus, Essex, 1963. Photo by SSPL / Getty Images.

Leisure time for men in the 1950s and 1960s was limited to Saturday afternoons and Sundays. Any spare time was spent socialising, growing vegetables and gardening. Other popular hobbies included model railways, golf, fishing, pigeon racing and watching sport.

Men Playing Bowls
Contributor: Chronicle / Alamy Stock Photo.

Watering Tomatoes
A former car factory worker, watering his tomato plants in his greenhouse 1957.
Photo by Jack Esten / Picture Post / Getty Images.

Homegrown beds of dahlias grow in the front garden of a council house in the early 1960s.
Contributor: RichardBaker / Alamy Stock Photo.

The 1950s and 1960s family home was very different from today. Housework was much more difficult, for example people did their washing by hand, instead of in a machine and with refrigerators being a luxury item for most people, food had to be bought daily.

Leisure time was limited for women, however they enjoyed knitting, baking, playing board games and meeting friends.

Young Woman Knitting At Home. Photo by Popperfoto / Getty Images.

English actress Violet Carson who plays the character of Ena Sharples in the television soap opera Coronation Street, pictured arranging cut flowers in a glass bowl in her garden at home, England, 1962.
Photo by Popperfoto / Getty Images.

Sometimes you will never know the value of a moment, until it becomes a memory.

Women on the Waltzers fair ride 1966.
Contributor: Trinity Mirror / Mirrorpix / Alamy Stock Photo.

Children having fun driving bumper cars at a fairground, 1960s.
Contributor: Allan Cash Picture Library / Alamy Stock Photo.

6

Board games and card games were a popular activity during the 1950s and 1960s. Many families played board games including Monopoly, Blow Football, Bucaneer, Mouse Trap, Cluedo, and Battleships.

Monopoly being played at home in Tooting, 1951. Photo by Maurice Ambler / Picture Post / Getty Images.

MONOPOLY

Graphic Design by Duncan Watts
Photo retouch by Studio 213

Published by
Pictures to Share
Community Interest Company.
Tattenhall, Cheshire
www.picturestoshare.co.uk

Printed in Europe through Beamreach Printing, Cheshire, UK

To see our other titles go to
www.picturestoshare.co.uk